MW01264534

ENDORSEMENTS

I believe that personal encounters with the Lord draw us to a deeper sense of intimacy with the Father. Learning how to position ourselves toward an encounter with the Lord is a fundamental part of our growth with Him. Dani has shared what a set of personal encounters can look like, hoping to motivate you toward greater intimacy with the Father. He loves you! Position your heart and let him speak to you.

MITCH IVEY
Senior Pastor, Grace Fellowship Church, Kearney, Nebraska

If there has been anytime in history when each of us needs a real encounter with a supernatural God, it is now. God never intended for us to have an unemotional, abstract relationship with Him. He continually wants to show us that He is more than philosophy, more than a theology, more than just some intellectual belief system. He is a loving Father who cares about every little detail of our lives. In Dani's devotional, she will challenge you to have a relationship with God that is alive and relevant. Each day's devotion will inspire you to expect and anticipate your own divine encounter with a loving Abba God as she transparently shares her own awesome experiences with God. I believe that this devotional will give you a revelation of who God is and how you too can have an exciting relationship with him. Get ready for the next thirty-one days of your life to become one of the most passionate love affairs of your life. God is waiting....

ROBERT CORBELL
Senior Pastor, River of Life Christian Center, Rusk, Texas

I really believe God the Father is calling His people into a greater realm of reality to confirm their faith and establish a deeper level of intimacy with them. *Journey Through the Door* is a 31-day glimpse into a walk of intimacy showing how God can reveal Himself through daily experiences in the heavenly realities we believe in. As her husband, I have personally walked with Dani through the season in which God began to reveal Himself to her, and I have marveled at the revelation, understanding, and healing these encounters brought to her and to our family in a very difficult season of our life and ministry. She is an amazing wife, mother, teacher, and worship leader and, in the midst of all the busyness of our lives, Father invited her to experience Him. Her experiences are an invitation for all of us to pray our eyes are opened, to come closer, and to take the journey through the door.

MITCH STRODA
Revival Revolution, Kearney, Nebraska

Journey Through the Door is an invitation to follow Dani on a journey. She designed this short devotional not to teach but rather to give a glimpse into her personal encounters with God. I love the real, raw, and unfiltered stories of the revelatory realm and the spiritual world. Its easy to imagine yourself sitting on a couch with a cup of coffee listening to Dani simply share her experience. I'm reminded of the apostle Paul in 2 Corinthians 12 when he was sharing about his heavenly encounters. He wasn't sure if he went to heaven in the body or in the spirit, but either way he'd never be the same. May you have similar life-changing encounters with God as you journey through the door.

JONATHAN LUMBARD
Lead Pastor, Spirit of Life Church, Kearney, Nebraska
Author of Sustaining Presence–creating a landing pad for the supernatural

Journey Through the Door
A 31-Day Devotional for Stepping into Heaven's Realities
Copyright © 2016—Dani Stroda

Unless otherwise identified, Scripture quotations are taken from The Voice Bible Copyright © 2012 Thomas Nelson, Inc. The Voice™ translation © 2012 Ecclesia Bible Society All rights reserved.

Scripture quotations marked MSG are taken from The Message, Copyright © 1993, 1994, 1995, 1996, 2000, 2001, 2002. Used by permission of NavPress Publishing Group. Scripture quotations marked NKJV are taken from the New King James Version, Copyright © 1982 by Thomas Nelson, Inc. Used by permission. All rights reserved. Scripture quotations marked HCSB are taken from the Holman Christian Standard Bible, Copyright © 1999, 2000, 2002, 2003, 2009 by Holman Bible Publishers, Nashville Tennessee. All rights reserved. Scripture quotations marked NLT are taken from the Holy Bible, New Living Translation, copyright© 1996, 2004, 2007, 2013 by Tyndale House Foundation. Used by permission of Tyndale House Publishers Inc., Carol Stream, Illinois 60188. All rights reserved. Scripture quotations marked ERV are taken from the Easy-to-Read Version, Copyright © 2006 by Bible League International. Scripture quotations marked GW are taken from the God's Word Translation, Copyright © 1995 by God's Word to the Nations. Used by permission of Baker Publishing Group. Scripture quotations marked WE are taken from the Worldwide English New Testament, © 1969, 1971, 1996, 1998 by SOON Educational Publications, Willington, Derby, DE65 6BN, England. Scripture quotations marked as TPT are taken from *The Psalms: Poetry on Fire, The Passion Translation*TM, copyright © 2012. Used by permission of Five Fold Media, LLC, Syracuse, NY 13039, United States of America. All rights reserved.

Editing Services: Aurora Writing & Editing Services www.aurora-pub.com
Cover Design and Interior design: Renee Evans Design reneeevansdesign.com

PO Box 1475
Kearney, NE 68848
www.revivalrevolution.life

ISBN 978-0-9966744-3-0

Printed in the United States of America

ACKNOWLEDGMENTS

Several books and teachers have helped me on my journey in the heavenly realms, including Ian Clayton, Blake Healy's *The Veil*, Wendy Alec's books, Frank Peretti's books, and C.S. Lewis' books.

DEDICATED TO...

MY HUSBAND
Mitch, thank you for choosing me to do life with. Your encouragement, support, and love has been invaluable as I press into all that Jesus has for me. I love you!

MY DAUGHTERS
Jaci, Chandler, Robin, and Journey:
Each one of you is amazing, and I can't believe I get to be your mamma. I am being shaped and molded into my full potential because of you all. I'm so proud of each one of you!

GRACE FELLOWSHIP AND THE GRACE SUPERNATURAL TRAINING SCHOOL
Thank you for being my tribe! I feel so blessed to get to partner with you all in influencing our city and the region for Jesus. Thank you for cultivating an environment that makes it easy for people to encounter Jesus. I'm forever grateful to you for loving our family so well.

Many thanks to KATIE ADAM for all her input, advice, and support in each step of the publishing process!

PREFACE

The goal of this little devotional is not to persuade you of the theological truth of our access to the heavenly (of heaven) or spiritual realm.[1] It's not to argue doctrine or even to teach extensively on the subject of heaven's realities. Instead, in this devotional I share my personal journey over the past few years, with the purpose of inviting you to join me. The Lord is standing at a heavenly door, beckoning us to experience the realities of His world.

Will you say *yes* to the journey?

Over and over, scripture tells us we have access to the heavenly realm. Many stories throughout the Old and New Testaments document others' experiences and invite us into similar experiences. In fact, an Old Testament story, in Second Kings, prompted the writing of this devotional. In it, the servant of the prophet Elisha woke up early and went outside. There he saw a great army, along with many horses and chariots, encircling the place where they were staying. Feeling terrified, the servant said to Elisha, *"Ah! Master, what are we going to do now?"*

Elisha responded, *"Have no fear. We have more on our side than they do."* Then he prayed to God, *"O Eternal One, I ask You to allow my servant to see heavenly realities."* Immediately, God

---

[1] I will use the words *heavenly* and *spiritual* interchangeably throughout this book.

opened Elisha's servant's spiritual eyes, and he saw heavenly horses and chariots of fire surrounding them (2 Kings 6:15–17). In this way, the servant was welcomed into Elisha's experience of the heavenly realm.

The heavenly realm is a reality that surrounds us; it is not just a destination in the sky after we die. I define *heavenly* or *spiritual realities* as "realities that are not of this world but of the heavenly or spiritual realm." Many believers live their entire Christian existence on this planet without being aware of what is happening in the heavenly realm. But I am convinced that the experiencing of spiritual realities is a gift the Lord wants to share with His people.

The Bible exhorts us to pursue God's gifts. Paul says, *"Passionately seek the gifts of the Spirit"* (1 Cor.14:1). I believe the ability to experience the spiritual realm is one of the gifts of the Spirit—a gift God offers to all of us. Since it is a gift from Him, we can trust Him to protect us and keep us from deception. He is a good gift-giver (see James 1:17).

Jesus explains it this way:

If your son asked you for bread, would you give him a stone? Of course not—you would give him a loaf of bread. If your son asked for a fish, would you give him a snake? No, to be sure, you would give him a fish—the best fish you could find. So if you, who are sinful, know how to give your children good gifts, how much more so does your Father in heaven, who is perfect, know how to give great gifts to His children (Matthew 7:9–11).

For lovers and followers of Jesus, encounters and experiences in the spiritual realm build on our intimacy with Him, helping us to know Him in a greater way. In this, they are an incredible gift.

To enrich your daily adventure into the world of encounters with Jesus, I have included daily scriptures that coincide with the encounter for the day. These are not meant to be taken out of context from the whole of the Scriptures or to validate my experiences in any way. Instead, I give them as an invitation to meditate on the truth of the Bible.

The spiritual world is God's world, and He wants to share it with us *before* we die and go to heaven. Will you join me on that journey?

INTRODUCTION

I invited Jesus into my heart at the age of seven at a Vacation Bible School at the Evangelical Free Church in Kearney, Nebraska. My mom, who had newly rededicated her life to the Lord, had begun taking my siblings and me to church with her. I vividly remember my experience of asking Jesus into my life. That day, He became a reality to me, and I began my love relationship with Him.

After my mom found out about my decision, she bought me a little daily devotional. In it was a place to write down prayer requests. That first day, I wrote my first prayer request—I wanted my daddy to get saved. The very next day, my dad had an encounter with the Lord and asked Him into His life! Seeing such a miracle within the first few days of my own salvation solidified my walk with Jesus like concrete. Ever since that experience, thirty years ago, I have never wavered in my love for Him. I've walked through some sketchy years, including a few years of rebellion in my heart against my parents. I'm certainly not perfect or without sin, but even in my hardest moments, Jesus never left me. I always kept close to Him because I felt loved by Him, even during the times when I was not very easy to love.

The Lord has always been very real to me. I have always believed in angels and the heavenly realm, but I don't remember seeing into that realm until I became an adult. I had relegated those gifts to people with the prophetic gifting or calling. I didn't think that was my gift, so I didn't think I could see into the heavenly realm. My gifting, from a very early age, was worship. I began leading worship when I was just fourteen, and it was the center of my ministry life until my early thirties. I loved leading people into encounters with the Father through worship. However, I personally had not experienced openly seeing into the heavenly realm or having heavenly encounters.

My journey of seeing spiritual realities began in 2010, when I attended the Bethel School of Kingdom Creativity at Bethel Church in Redding, California. A friend had invited me to go with her, and though I didn't feel like I had much creativity in me, I wanted to go because I wanted to visit Bethel Church again. My family had been there just earlier that year, and we had fallen in love with the atmosphere of the church and the presence of Jesus there.

During the few days of the school, instead of only growing in my worship experience, which I assumed was my only creative outlet, I found fun in finger painting. I went to a workshop with Trisha Wheeler, where she had us paint blindfolded. This terrified me and I started to panic, until the Lord told me, "Use your fingers instead of a brush and have fun!" In that simple experience, God started to break off some of the fear in my life and open up the spiritual realm to me.

While at the school, I also received several prophetic drawings from people. The drawings I received encouraged me greatly. They were just little sketches of what these people had seen in me, yet each one had significance. I often look at these prophetic pictures and remember the encouragement and promises of the Lord for me. I came home from this experience with instructions from the Lord to "draw what you see." He wanted me to begin drawing prophetic pictures, too. So, armed with a new sketch pad and some crayons, I began to do just that.

I started sketching little pictures or writing words—whatever I saw. These were not usually things to share with anyone. I was just practicing seeing into the spiritual realm and then putting it on paper. My drawings were not very good (artistically speaking), but they were the beginning of my journey.

The season of drawing what I saw eventually trickled off into an inconsistent habit. I had also begun to occasionally have dreams, and I tried to write them in my journal. Though I was not very consistent with it, the idea of drawing or writing what I saw had become more important to me, and my journaling became a little less erratic than it had been in the past.

Then, in January of 2013, I had an encounter with God that began the next phase of my journey. Because it was the beginning of a new year, I was seeking the Lord for what He had for me that year. One morning, He began to speak to me about experiencing greater spiritual realities. I noticed a spot on the wall that seemed to sparkle, and it caused me to think about a portal into the heavenly realms. God then told me He had experiences for me that He wanted to begin that year. My first thoughts were of the New Age and the weird things they get into. I didn't (and still don't) want to veer from God into anything that is sent from the enemy instead of initiated by God. Thankfully, God spoke to my fears and told me I needed to trust Him. I must not let fear hold me back. He reminded me that He is so much bigger than the enemy, and if I would trust Him, He would take me into realities beyond what I had ever imagined. In response I said, "I will go there with You."

I did not have an immediate flood of experiences, but gradually, they began. Sometimes I would close my eyes, see Him somewhere, and step into that reality with Him. Many times, He would give me a revelation about some truth. At other times (He had to teach me this), the goal was to just have fun and enjoy the experience with Him, without any lesson.

Writing this devotional does not mean I have arrived. I am still growing and looking forward to greater experiences of spiritual realities. I don't have encounters daily, but I try to maintain an open heart and spirit to whatever and wherever the Lord has for me.

It is a journey—one I hope you will join me on. Let's step through the door together!

GETTING STARTED

Before you dive into this journey, here are a few simple tips to help you maximize this devotional.

1. FIND YOUR PLACE.

Our Heavenly Father is omnipresent. He is everywhere. He can encounter us anywhere. He is always around us, even when we aren't aware of His presence. It isn't necessary to have a certain place to meet with God; however, for the purposes of beginning this journey, I encourage you to choose a meeting place. Maybe you already have a designated place where you read your Bible and pray. Or maybe it's somewhere new every time you meet with Him. Maybe you have never had a specific place. No matter what your past routine has or hasn't been, find a place to position yourself to encounter His presence over these next thirty-one days. Invite Him to join you at a specific location, to encounter you, and to flood you with His heavenly realities.

2. SET THE ATMOSPHERE.

Again, God is always everywhere and needs no special environment to encounter you. But, you may want to use the tool of music to help you engage with Him and increase your awareness of Him. I love worship music. In this season, I have especially enjoyed Bethel Music and Jesus Culture. Having music playing usually helps me to connect with the Lord faster and easier. The same may be true for you. Decide whether you want to find music—perhaps something instrumental that doesn't distract you—to help create an environment where it is easy for you to encounter the Lord.

3. SEE THIS AS A DOORWAY.

My goal in writing this devotional is to help open up spiritual realities to you. Each day for the next thirty-one days, you will read one of my past encounters with the Lord. Some are short and vague; some are longer and full of detail. Look at each daily reading as a doorway to step through into your own heavenly experiences with the Lord. Maybe you've had lots of encounters with the Lord. Or maybe the idea kind of freaks you out. Wherever you are at on this journey, give any fear you may feel to the Lord. Let His love overwhelm you, because perfect love casts our fear. Then declare your trust for Him, saying, "I will go there with You." You will be amazed by what He will show you.

A private place is reserved for the lovers of God where they receive revelation-secrets of His promises.

PSALM 25:14 TPT

DAY 1

I see myself before our Creator, Daddy God, in a large room—perhaps the Throne Room written about in scripture. There, I'm making a sacrifice—kneeling down and laying down the small thing I had in my hands. Sadness grips my heart, but I know that what I'm doing is required, so I leave my gift at the altar and turn to walk away.

Daddy God calls me back and gives me a gift, a ginormous box. I had laid down a small sacrifice, and He rewards me with a much larger gift. I am shocked, but then I wonder if I must immediately give this gift on the sacrificial altar as well. Daddy God shakes His head. No, this gift is for me to keep. I get to take it along with me.

I turn again to leave. I start out the way I came, down the path I feel like I have always taken. Then, someone—I'm not sure who—tells me I must take the other path. I start to argue until I hear that this gift I'm carrying will not fit down the worn path I've always taken. That path is narrow, and what I am now carrying is much too wide. So now, I must take the wide path.

May the Eternal repay you for your sacrifices and reward you richly for what you have done. It is under the wings of Israel's God, the Eternal One, that you have sought shelter.

RUTH 2:12

WHAT I SAW...

DAY 2

I am alone, or so I think, as I walk down the wide path. Then, I discover I've been enveloped by something like fairy dust, but it's a living, moving being. It surrounds me and follows me, like a trail of colorful, floating glitter. I remember Psalm 23:6 and realize this being is the embodiment of Goodness and Mercy, who are promised to follow me all the days of my life.

As I walk along, suddenly my box, the gift from Daddy God, pops open, startling me. Fireworks and confetti fly everywhere. It's a big moment, an intense moment. I begin to fall backward, but before I hit the ground, Goodness and Mercy catch me. Then I notice people all around me. They've been watching me walk the path, juggling this big box. As they have watched, they've whispered to each other, asking *why* I am carrying this big unopened box. When the box suddenly pops open, the whispering stops.

In this moment, I begin to feel stunned and overwhelmed. I feel like I need to sit down, to retreat. I hear Holy Spirit tell me I can go rest in my cave of solitude if I want, but only for a while. I can rest until I get my joy back. I must have lost it in the intensity of the moment. I can rest in this hidden place until my joy returns; then I will journey on. Everything—the path, Goodness and Mercy, the gift—will all be right here when I return from my cave. I look around and see my cave where I hadn't noticed it before, just to the side of the path. I go in, and I rest.

He reached down and drew me from the deep, dark hole where I was stranded, mired in the muck and clay. With a gentle hand, He pulled me out to set me down safely on a warm rock; He held me until I was steady enough to continue the journey again.

PSALM 40:2

WHAT I SAW...

DAY 3

I find myself standing on a massive battleship with Jesus. We walk the deck, and He leads me into different areas with all kinds of supplies. One room is filled with bags of blood for the wounded who need life. The next room has tools like scalpels, needles, and thread for stitches. Sometimes surgery is needed to remove spiritual disease and tumors. Daddy God is a gracious surgeon, exact and precise, knowing exactly what's needed and when surgery must happen.

Then, Jesus takes me into a strange room filled with piles and piles of rocks. I am confused. The blood bags and surgeon's tools make sense—but rocks? The rocks are white and smooth, and I see no markings. But then, Jesus picks one up and turns it around to show me it has a name on it. I immediately think of Revelation 2:17, *"I will... give you a white stone. Upon this stone, a new name is engraved. No one knows this name except for its recipient."* Now it makes sense.

When we come to Daddy God for healing, when He does surgery and fills us with life, He also gives us a new name. Engraved on a white stone, it is a special secret between us and Him. We enter broken, but we leave healed. We leave with a new name, a new identity.

And I will give to each one a white stone, and on the stone will be engraved a new name that no one understands except the one who receives it.

REVELATION 2:17 NLT

WHAT I SAW...

DAY 4

I find myself in a forest. The massive and abundant trees are suffocating. I need out. Beginning to panic, I weave in and out through the trees, trying to find my way out. Instead, with every turn I seem to go deeper into the dark forest. I feel myself starting to hyperventilate. Then I hear Daddy God's voice—"SIT!" The command booms between the trees. "Wait," He says, "and I will show you the path. There is a path. Sit down and you'll see the path. It will be lit up for you."

I obey. I sit and wait. Then, suddenly, I turn and notice a picnic set up before me. David's words echo in my mind: *"You prepare a table before me in the presence of my enemies"* (Ps. 23:5 NKJV). Peace returns. Now, I can sit still and trust Him.

Your word is a lamp to my feet and a light to my path.
PSALM 119:105 NKJV

WHAT I SAW...

DAY 5

My family and I are in our home, doing life together. Suddenly, the wind begins to blow so hard that our home begins to move. I look out the window and see that our house is racing like a car down the interstate. It seems like we "drive" down the road forever. Standing by the window, I watch the fields pass by.

Finally, we come to a stop. I tell my kids, "Go look out the window. We are now in a new place. In a new neighborhood." We all walk out of the house and sit in the grass, wondering about the strange events. I look up at the sky, where I see a bright light. It seems familiar. *I've seen this light before*, I think to myself. Then, I notice something in the light—a dove.

I'm startled as the dove touches down and lights a stick on fire. The stick is now my torch, which radiates from my home that's in a new place.

One day, the Eternal One called out to Abram. Eternal One: Abram, get up
and go! Leave your country. Leave your relatives and your father's home,
and travel to the land I will show you. Don't worry—I will guide you there.
GENESIS 12:1

WHAT I SAW...

DAY 6

We are sitting on the beach, Jesus and me. We sit on the sand, eating funnel cakes and watching the waves in silence. We do this for a long time. Finally, we get up and begin to walk down the beach. Some of my favorite times with Him are on this beach. We walk for a while until we come across a raft. It is a surprise to me, but He, of course, knew it was there all along. We get on the raft and began to float out to sea. The sun is setting beautifully on the horizon. Suddenly, I realize we have a picnic basket between us. Jesus opens it and hands me something to drink.

I ask Him, "Why is there always food when we are together?"

His answer melts my heart. "I know how much you enjoy food." He knows me so well.

And so we have bread to make our bodies strong, wine to make our heart happy, oil to make our faces shine. Every good thing we need, Your earth provides.

Genesis 12:1

WHAT I SAW...

DAY 7

I am on a ship with Jesus. This time it is not a raft, gently floating on the seas, but a large ship reminiscent of a pirate ship. We are moving quickly across the water, and I can sense that enemy ships are not far away. Jesus tells me we are in dangerous seas, with enemies nearby, and we are heading to an island. A person is stranded there and has been surviving there, alone, for too long. Thus, Jesus and I are on a rescue mission—to bring back the one.

As we near the island, I realize more people are on the ship with us. In fact, we have a whole crew. We are a large group, all going to rescue the one. I think of the scripture where Jesus the Shepherd leaves the ninety-nine to find and rescue the one (see Matt. 18:12). I feel in awe of the fact that this time Jesus is actually taking the ninety-nine with Him to rescue the one.

We arrive at the island and storm the shores to find the weary one, who has been surviving in a dangerous land alone. The rescue squad has finally come. We find and surround the one—offering love, encouragement, help, comfort, and support. The weary survivor has been rescued. The many went out to rescue the one.

May the Eternal's answer find you, come to rescue you, when you desperately cling to the end of your rope.

PSALM 20:1

WHAT I SAW...

DAY 8

I am on a raft with God—a raft made of logs tied together with rope. It is rugged and antique looking. We are floating down a gentle river. I wonder whether the water will stay calm and gentle or if we are heading toward rapids or falls. I will not be disappointed by a wild ride, as long as I am on the raft with Him. I am ready for an adventure. He knows my thoughts and says, "We're going to stay on the lazy river for a while." I am OK with that, too. I had been feeling like I needed some "lazy" time. Evidently, I did.

As we lie there, side by side, just floating along, I look over and realize it is the Holy Spirit with me. Usually, my adventures are led by Jesus—my friend and brother. Today, Holy Spirit, my Comforter and Nurturer, is sharing this experience with me. I notice a name etched into the side of one of the raft's logs— *Selah*. Yes, it is time for a pause, floating down the lazy river on the Selah.

Thus God blessed day seven and made it special—an open time for pause and restoration, a sacred zone of Sabbath-keeping, because God rested from all the work He had done in creation that day.

GENESIS 2:3

WHAT I SAW...

DAY 9

I am sitting in a bed of flowers, but I am as small as a bumblebee. It feels like a scene from *Lord of the Rings* or another fantasy, where humans exist alongside giants. Sitting on a flower petal, in a daze, I am only half awake. Suddenly, a being comes and wraps me up in what seems like a large lettuce leaf. The being then puts me on a giant flying bug, like a dragonfly. I wonder if I should be afraid, but deep down I know I can trust the one in control of my adventure. I am not sure what is happening, where I am, or where I am going, but I know I can trust.

Jehoshaphat bowed his head low, and all the assembly fell prostrate before the Eternal and worshiped Him with reverence. They trusted the Lord completely.

2 CHRONICLES 20:18

WHAT I SAW...

DAY 10

I am sitting on a sandy island under a palm tree with Jesus, and I am chewing on a stalk of wheat that dangles from my lips. Instead of beach clothes, I am wearing a trendy outfit, something one would not normally wear on the beach. Jesus and I are sipping Coke, laughing big belly laughs, and totally enjoying each other's fellowship. Each part of this scene represents part of who I am. I love the islands. My home is in the Midwest, surrounded by the beauty of farm country. I tend to dress according to urban trends. And whenever I am with friends, we always enjoy food and drink.

Suddenly, a red carpet rolls out along the beach straight toward a cruise ship anchored several dozen yards away. Jesus links arms with me, like an usher at a wedding, and we walk on the red carpet toward the ship. Once on the ship, I see that it is filled with all kinds of fun activities! One can enjoy dancing, bowling, tennis, or basketball, and in the pampering rooms, one can get massages, pedicures, and manicures. The bottom of the ship even has a glass section, so one can sit and watch the fish swim below. I jump into all the activities, always with Jesus or the Holy Spirit at my side. Sometimes the three of us play together. Every once in a while, Daddy God joins in, too—like when we play tennis and need a fourth person. I am never having fun alone; God is always by my side. All this is happening—all the fun and enjoyment—on the ship while we are anchored at the shore.

...so we threw out the sea anchor to slow us down.
ACTS 27:17B

WHAT I SAW...

DAY 11

Jesus and I are walking in what looks like the remains of a forest. Dead trees and dead leaves are everywhere. Not one thing has a touch of green left on it. Brown, dark, and desolate—the place looks like a fire swept through. I feel sad that, though Jesus is walking through this place, it has no life. I ask Him, "Can this place come alive?" He looks at me as though I should answer my own question. I'm not sure if He tells me to do this or if His look stirs something within me, but I find myself speaking to the nearest dead tree. "Come alive. Come alive." Slowly, life returns as I coax it with my words. It is like a movie in slow motion. As I watch, the tree comes alive and grows green leaves.

I move to the next dead tree. This time, Jesus tells me to put my hand on the tree as I speak. Life comes a little quicker. He is teaching me how to bring life to dead things. As we crunch on the dead leaves, moving to the next lifeless tree, I feel like I should dance. I half-skip along, and the leaves beneath me began to green up, coming alive. Before I even touch the next tree, life begins to come. My dancing emanates life.

What began as a half-hearted skip becomes an extravagant full-motion dance as I move along. Life springs up all around me. Suddenly, I am wearing professional dancewear—a leotard and flowing skirt—as I effortlessly glide through the forest. Then, I become a young child, dancing innocently, bringing life as I go.

So I did what God told me to do: I prophesied to the breath. As I was speaking, breath invaded the lifeless. The bodies came alive and stood on their feet.

EZEKIEL 37:10

WHAT I SAW...

DAY 5

"Then, I notice something in the light—a dove."

DAY 10

"I am sitting on a sandy island under a palm tree with Jesus..."

DAY 19
"Jesus invites me to sit on another swing..."

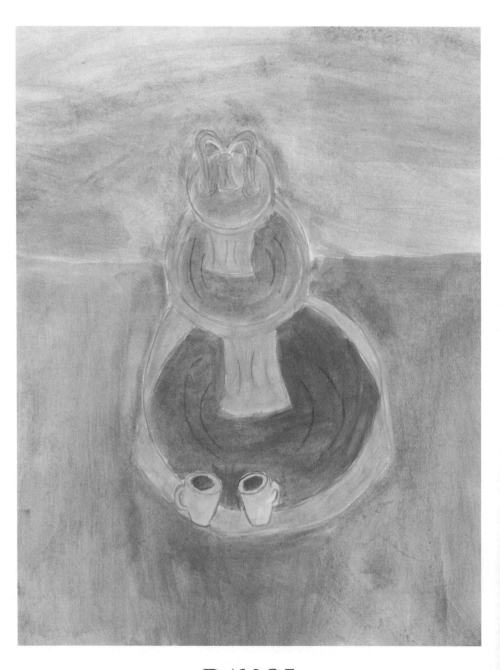

DAY 25

"Jesus and I both have a cup of coffee..."

DAY 12

I am with Daddy God in a bubble, like a snow globe. The noise of the world is all around, but in the protection of the bubble, we are oblivious and can't hear a thing. In the bubble, we are sitting in a garden surrounded by flowers. Instead of snow, glitter floats all around us. I see musical notes floating, too. It is as though we are singing, and our song becomes visible and fills the bubble. It is a peaceful place, within the noise and chaos of the world but, at the same time, separate from it.

I'm telling you these things while I'm still living with you. The Friend, the Holy Spirit whom the Father will send at my request, will make everything plain to you. He will remind you of all the things I have told you. I'm leaving you well and whole. That's my parting gift to you. Peace. I don't leave you the way you're used to being left—feeling abandoned, bereft. So don't be upset. Don't be distraught.

JOHN 14:27 MSG

WHAT I SAW...

DAY 13

I find myself in a rainforest so thick I can't see light coming from anywhere. I begin to move. I have to find my way out. Jesus isn't nearby. Neither is the Holy Spirit. I can't sense His presence at all. I hate this feeling. I need to get out. *Where is He?* I keep moving forward, unsure of whether I am even moving in the right direction. Sometimes it is hard, and I want to sit down and cry. But no, I need to keep moving. Surely I can find Him if I keep moving. It seems like forever, but finally a space opens up, and there He is. Though we are still in the rainforest, it is no longer thick and suffocating. Here we are in an open space.

He begins to speak to me, telling me He is so proud of me for searching for Him, for refusing to sit and wait in fear or frustration. He is thrilled that I pursued Him. He says He knew that I would, and I did. He is so happy.

Even if I am afraid and think to myself, "There is no doubt that the darkness will swallow me, the light around me will soon be turned to night." You can see in the dark, for it is not dark to Your eyes. For You the night is just as bright as the day. Darkness and light are the same to Your eyes.

PSALM 139:11–12

WHAT I SAW...

DAY 14

I am working on a farm with Jesus. I hate the dirty, hard work, and I tell Him so: "I hate this, Lord." Looking around, I see such a mess, and I hate the work.

He tells me, "That's because you're looking at it wrong. You need to make it fun." His words echo the lecture of many a mother. I think of the children's song, "Clean up, clean up..." which tries to make a boring task into fun and easy work. I don't know how to make this work fun. To me, it is gross and not at all fun.

Suddenly, Jesus chucks a handful of mud at me. I want to be mad at Him, but how can I be? He starts running, and I chase Him. Before I know it, I am laughing and having fun. "You see?" He says. "Make it fun."

I tell Him this is fun, but our play isn't finishing the work that needs to be done. As I speak, I look behind me and realize the work is done. Somehow, in the throwing of mud and the running and laughing, our work was completed.

But his answer was: "My grace is all you need, for my power is greatest when you are weak."

2 Corinthians 12:9 GNT

WHAT I SAW...

DAY 15

I am in the yard of a house surrounded by a white picket fence. It is my home, but a very whimsical, fairy tale–like home. From my yard, pacing behind the fence, I watch the outside world. Pacing, pacing, pacing. I can't see Him, but I feel Daddy God in my yard with me.

Just when it seems like I have paced the fence forever, I finally stop at the gate, unlock it, and walk out. Once out, instead of walking, I begin to run down the middle of the street. I run from one end of town to the other and then back again, with a big grin on my face. I am enjoying the run. The wind is blowing through my hair, and I do not feel tired. Looking around, I notice I am running with a small crowd, maybe ten or fifteen others. We run down the street, from one end to the other, running as fast as we can. Again, I can't see Him, but I feel Daddy God near me, all around me, as we run.

Eventually, I stop at my house. I go through the gate and sit down on the patio furniture in my yard. Though I do not feel tired from the running, I am resting now. I look at Daddy God, asking Him silently if I will run again. "Oh yes," I feel Him whisper. "Now that you have gone through the gate the first time, you can go in and out as you want."

But those who trust in the Eternal One will regain their strength. They will soar on wings as eagles. They will run—never winded, never weary. They will walk—never tired, never faint.

ISAIAH 40:31

WHAT I SAW...

DAY 16

I am at a fence again, but not a picket fence and not in my yard. This time I am in the country, and a rickety wooden fence separates a pasture from a dirt road. I stand with Daddy God, Jesus, and the Holy Spirit in the pasture, leaning on the fence, looking out at the road. When someone walks by, we wave, chat a minute, and hand the person a Coca-Cola. Another person walks by a bit later, and then another. Sometimes the conversation is short; sometimes the person stays a while and even greets others with us. Always, as the people leave, we give them a can of Coke. Some people run by, with no time for a chat, but we run a Coke out to them just the same. For hours, we continue our mission, making sure everyone who passes by receives a can of Coke.

Reliable friends who do what they say are like cool drinks in sweltering heat—refreshing!
PROVERBS 25:13 MSG

WHAT I SAW...

DAY 17

I seem to be in some sort of whimsical fairytale land. It is half-playground, half-carnival, and pastel colors rule. I see life-size dumdum suckers, a merry-go-round, a cotton candy booth, a slide. The atmosphere radiates with a soft, delight-filled aura.

I enjoy a whirl on the merry-go-round and then run toward the slide, having such a good time. Suddenly, I realize that just outside this fairytale land is a thick darkness filled with blindfolded women. They are grasping around in the darkness, with no idea that, for some of them, they are just inches away from a different life, free of blindfolds and darkness. This land of freedom, fun, and brightness is completely different from their dark world.

I feel Daddy God prompting me to grab the arm of a woman and pull her into this different reality. I run out into the darkness, grab her arm, and pull her into this whimsical place. She is changed forever. She begins to enjoy the merry-go-round, to get cotton candy, to have fun. Now, it is time to rescue another woman from the eerie, dark world and bring her into this pastel and whimsical light. I run out again, grabbing another woman by her arm and pulling her into this better and brighter reality. I do this over and over. It is never a violent rescue but always a swift one. I simply run out intentionally toward one woman and pull her into our fairytale world.

Or do you despise the riches of His kindness, restraint, and patience, not recognizing that God's kindness is intended to lead you to repentance?

ROMANS 2:4 HCSB

WHAT I SAW...

DAY 18

I have water skis on and am standing in the clouds, holding a rope. Looking ahead of me to see what kind of vehicle is going to pull me through the clouds, I see a big white horse! He starts to gallop across the clouds, pulling me behind him. Jesus is standing to the side, watching me fly across the clouds, just like a water skier flies across the water. I jump a "ramp," only to realize it is actually an airplane! After that, I jump several more airplanes. We are going so fast and having so much fun. Jesus and I are both laughing hysterically.

Then, the scene switches into slow motion, like the climax of a movie, where anticipation builds for what is going to happen next. Jesus and the horse seem to be having a conversation about whether I am ready to handle the next jump. I look ahead. Instead of another airplane I see a set of mountain peaks. It is the jump of a lifetime. The horse speeds up, and I brace myself. Still in slow motion, I ramp up the mountains and fly for what seems like forever. When I finally land, I falter and, for a moment, think I am falling. But I regain my balance. I did it. I conquered the epic jump!

Then I saw heaven open, and I saw a white horse! The One who rode him is called "One who can be Trusted" and "The True One". He punishes and makes war in the right way.

REVELATION 19:11 WE

WHAT I SAW...

DAY 19

I find Jesus sitting on a swing that hangs from a branch. As I look closer, I see that it isn't a tree branch but the Cross. Jesus invites me to sit on another swing that hangs from the other arm of the Cross. He tells me that too many people view the Cross only as a place of repentance, but it is also the place of freedom. We leave our mess at the foot of the Cross, but He also wants to give us something. We should never leave the Cross empty-handed. As Jesus and I begin to swing, I discover that these are not ordinary swings. They are more like a ride at an amusement park. As we swing, the arms of the Cross begin to spin and twist like a helicopter propeller. As we swing faster and higher, the top of the Cross lifts off, and we spin up into the air. Then we fall back to earth. Then we are lifted up again, this time higher. We fall back again. Each time we are lifted, we go higher. I love the air blowing through my hair, the feeling of weightlessness as we swing into the air. I am experiencing freedom at the Cross.

Christ has made us really free. So, stay free! Do not let yourselves be made slaves again.

GALATIANS 5:1 WE

WHAT I SAW...

DAY 20

I am walking through a field. Out of nowhere, a swarm of mean black birds begins to dive down and peck at me. I start to run, and the birds chase me. Then a huge white eagle swoops down and covers me, like a full-body umbrella, as I continue to run. I'm not sure where we are headed, but I know it's a place of safety. The black birds continue to chase me, but they cannot touch me because of the eagle's protection. As we run, because I am now protected, the eagle and I begin to laugh. The atmosphere changes. Instead of the fear of being attacked, I feel as though I am just running from a storm to reach a dry a place. Finally, we arrive at a castle. Crossing the mote, we wait for the gate to open and let us in. Once we are in, I am free from the attacks of the black birds.

I want to live in your tent forever. I want to hide where you can protect me.
PSALM 61:4 ERV

WHAT I SAW...

DAY 21

I am swimming in a big pool of popcorn. Knowing this experience isn't about popcorn, I ask Daddy God, "What is this?" He tells me the popcorn symbolizes revelation— revelation of the word I have heard taught and have read in books, good revelation of the Kingdom of God. Then I come across a burnt piece of popcorn in my pool of good popcorn. Daddy God shows me I don't need to worry about false teaching or revelation because I will be able to tell it is bad (or burnt) and simply throw it out. I don't need to live in fear of false teaching, because I will know the difference—just as anyone who has eaten popcorn can tell the good popcorn from the burnt popcorn.

Then, I find myself swimming in a pool of unpopped popcorn kernels. Daddy God tells me this is a pool of my own revelation. The oil of the Holy Spirit, which fills me, will pop these kernels. These are the truths that will be revealed to me from His word and His voice. His truth will pop in my heart because of the oil of the Holy Spirit in me.

The seed cast on good earth is the person who hears and takes in the News, and then produces a harvest beyond his wildest dreams.

MATTHEW 13:23 MSG

WHAT I SAW...

DAY 22

I see an altar with smoke rising from it. Jesus and I are in the Throne Room before Daddy God, standing before my altar. Around us are rows of other altars belonging to other people. On my altar, I see piles of gifts. This is the altar where I put my sacrifices to Daddy God. As I receive gifts, I throw them back onto the altar before Daddy God. Amazingly, the gifts on the altar rise and disappear in the smoke, but then another gift rains down on me out of the smoke. I realize it is a cycle. I give what I have to Him; He takes it; and He rains more down on me. I think of Matthew 13:12—*"Those who have something will be given more—and they will have abundance"* Until recently, this verse had confused me. Now, I am beginning to see what it means.

I notice that at the other altars people also have gifts. Some put the gifts on the altar and experience the cycle of offering and receiving. Others hold their gifts, not willing to part with them. Ironically, the gifts soon disappear in their hands. They lose them anyway. In this place, one cannot hold onto things too long before one loses them. As the other half of the verse says, *"Those who have nothing will lose what they have—they will be destitute."* We watch this cycle continue. Then Jesus takes my hand, telling me the process will go on. I don't have to stand at my altar to engage it, because heavenly realms are different than the earthly realm. So, we run to an ocean, where we find a merry-go-round ride. I jump on, and Jesus spins me. As I spin on top of the water, I laugh with Jesus.

Those who have something will be given more—and they will have abundance. Those who have nothing will lose what they have—they will be destitute.

MATTHEW 13:12

WHAT I SAW...

DAY 23

Jesus and I are walking toward a huge tree with a tire swing hanging from it. When we reach it, I jump on the swing. He pushes me around and around, higher and higher. It is thrilling! I don't feel afraid, but I wonder how I can go so high without the tire swing coming loose from the tree. I look up. I see that the rope from the swing is not only wrapped several times around the massive branch but that it also has an anchor latched around the branch. The tire swing is anchored to the tree. I look below to see the tree's huge, deep roots. Several anchors are also deep into the ground. I am anchored, deeply anchored.

This hope is a strong and trustworthy anchor for our souls. It leads us through the curtain into God's inner sanctuary.

HEBREWS 6:19 NLT

WHAT I SAW...

DAY 24

I see myself in a life-size maze. At first, I think of a corn maze, but then I realize it is a maze of mirrors. I am not sure why I am there or what it means, but I follow it for a bit, and I keep thinking, *Everywhere you go, there you are.* I am not sure if this is a positive or a negative. I ask Daddy God for clarification. I ask Him if we are going anywhere else, but I hear nothing.

Now we see a blurred image in a mirror. Then we will see very clearly. Now my knowledge is incomplete. Then I will have complete knowledge as God has complete knowledge of me.

1 CORINTHIANS 13:12 GW

WHAT I SAW...

DAY 25

Jesus and I are sitting at a square table in a city park with a Scrabble board in front of us. The park has a big fountain, grassy hills, and a sidewalk circling and weaving through it. People are walking and sitting, enjoying the peace of the place. Jesus and I both have a cup of coffee, and I am thoroughly enjoying my relaxing time with Him. I say, "I could stay here forever."

He looks at me inquisitively. His eye seems to gleam. "What is forever?" He asks.

Why is He asking me such a ridiculous question? I wonder. I attempt an answer: "You know, for all time."

"There is no 'all time,'" He says. "We are in time."

I have no idea what He means, but it doesn't matter. Next, I randomly think I would really like a piece of cherry cheesecake. A second later, a being (perhaps an angel?) arrives by my side with a plate of cherry cheesecake. I am shocked. I had not said a word about wanting this. I ask Jesus about it, and He tells me, "Your thoughts are known. When you think something, it comes to pass." What a place we are in!

And I know God has made everything beautiful for its time. God has also placed in our minds a sense of eternity; we look back on the past and ponder over the future, yet we cannot understand the doings of God.

ECCLESIASTES 3:11

WHAT I SAW...

DAY 26

I am lying in a field of flowers with Jesus. We are both holding glasses of wine. Where there are flowers and fruity drinks, there are bees, too. But these bees aren't like earthly bees that one might fear or swat away. They don't pester us. They are just flying around, along with some hummingbirds.

When I spend time with Jesus, our conversations are usually light-hearted, involving lots of belly laughs. Today, however, seems to be more sacred and intimate. We enter a tender moment, and I know someone is about to say something solemn and sweet. I'm unsure whether this is my role or His. We sit in silence for a few minutes. Then He says, "I adore you." This catches me off guard. Usually, those are words I sing to Him. As we sit quietly, I let the impact of His words—His declaration of His adoration of me—sink in. Then He adds, "I'm devoted to you." I feel overwhelmed! *Adore* means "to like or admire very much," and *devoted* means "zealous or ardent in attachment, loyalty, or affection." *He adores me and is devoted to me!* I will cherish this tender moment forever.

Him (to her): You, my love are beautiful. So beautiful!
SONG OF SONGS 4:1

WHAT I SAW...

DAY 27

I am travelling down a road with Jesus. The road is paved, but it winds through rustic scenery. We are riding in a vehicle—similar to a golf cart—built for paved, smooth roads. Eventually, we hit a dead end. The paved road stops, and the terrain ahead looks rugged, muddy, and wild. I think this must be the end of our journey, since it's the end of the road. I wonder if the dead end means I chose the wrong direction to travel. But I am wrong. "Hitting a dead end does not always mean the journey is over or you've gone the wrong way," Jesus says. "Often, you are going in the right direction, and the dead end means you need a different vehicle to take on the adventure." Then, we jump into a large four-wheeler equipped with huge mudding tires. This dead end is not the end of the journey, but an invitation to go exploring in new places.

Yet the journey of the righteous has been charted by the Eternal.

PSALM 1:6

WHAT I SAW...

DAY 28

Jesus and I are in a cave, but it is no ordinary cave. Instead of being made from rock, it is made from jewels. As we journey quickly through the cave, we are climbing over boulders and stalagmites of amber jewels. We go on like this for a long time. Then the jewel changes, and now we are climbing through a ruby cave. We go along for a while, not saying much, just climbing through and over the jewel rocks. Again, the jewel changes; now, it is diamond. Finally, we arrive in a wide open part of the cave. It is like a normal cave of stone, but the whole room is filled with piles of gold and treasure. We sit down in the midst of the treasure to rest and take a drink. Because we climbed and crawled through the cave so far and so quickly, we are a bit worn out.

Later, I ask Jesus about the meaning of this experience. The sense I had, while we were in the cave, was one of mystery and mysticism, not fear but unknowingness. I Google *amber* (because we were in the amber halls the longest) and find that it can represent the presence of God. I feel that the long traveling through and over the amber represents being saturated with His presence. It's like each segment of the cave marks me. I don't have to pick up any stones or gold and carry them; they rub off on me so my skin actually glows with the substance of that stone. The most prevalent is the presence of God. Even in the room of gold, I know I am not going to take any of the treasure with me, away from this place. However, it also has marked me and become part of who I am.

He has enlightened us to the great mystery at the center of His will. With immense pleasure, He laid out His intentions through Jesus.

EPHESIANS 1:9

WHAT I SAW...

DAY 29

At first I don't know where I am; I just know Jesus and I are walking and eating hotdogs. Then, the view opens up and I see that we are walking through what looks like a county fair. For a while, we are just walking through the fairgrounds, eating our hotdogs and chatting about who knows what. Then Jesus leads me to the door of one of the buildings, and we walk in together. It is the horse stable. As we walk into the huge stable, it becomes an even bigger open pasture. We watch the horses as they gallop around, playing in the wide field. Though we are standing on the edge of the field, it is as if we have a close up camera view of the horses as they run. We can see their eyes and the way their manes blow in the wind. I think this must not be an earthly place.

After watching the horses for a while, we continue our walk through the fairgrounds. The next building Jesus leads me into is full of rabbits, like what 4-H kids would show at a county fair. But these are no ordinary rabbits. They are huge and fluffy. When Jesus holds one in His arms and then lets it hop away, it leaps about fifteen feet. We enjoy watching the rabbits hop around for a while. None of them are in cages. Then we continue our walk.

You shall walk in all the ways which the Lord your God has commanded you, that you may live and that it may be well with you, and that you may prolong your days in the land which you shall possess.

DEUTERONOMY 5:33 NKJV

WHAT I SAW...

DAY 30

Jesus and I are walking through the grass. We are tiny—as though we have been shrunk. The grass towers above us like tall trees. We reach a mound of rocks, which is like mountain terrain for us, considering our size. As we begin climbing through the rocky hills, I ask Jesus how He made Himself (and me) small like this. His answer is profound and echoes in my being—"I am who I want to become." He is who He is and who He wants to be.

Eternal One: I AM WHO I AM.
Exodus 3:14

WHAT I SAW...

DAY 31

I close my eyes and ask Jesus if He wants to take me somewhere. Instead of a vision, I hear His voice asking me, "Where do you want to go?"

A bit taken off-guard, I finally say, "Somewhere mystical and amazing." He asks if I want to go to the Temple. Of course I say yes.

We start walking toward massive golden stairs that lead to an enormous structure. The front lawn is like a park, a beautiful, heavenly park. As we walk down the lane toward the stairs, at certain spots our footsteps set off water fountains that surround the temple. Each water fountain has a different shooting design and height. It is creative, amazing, and extravagant. As we get closer, I see lion statues on either side of the staircase. Instead of stone, they are made of solid gold. The atmosphere surrounding the Temple is not light-hearted, but it's not somber, either. It is mystical. We climb the golden stairs, and Jesus opens the door.

All who ask receive. Those who seek, find what they seek. And he who knocks, will have the door opened.

MATTHEW 7:8

WHAT I SAW...